The Mystery of Freemasonry

An Educational Masonic Puzzle and Quiz Book

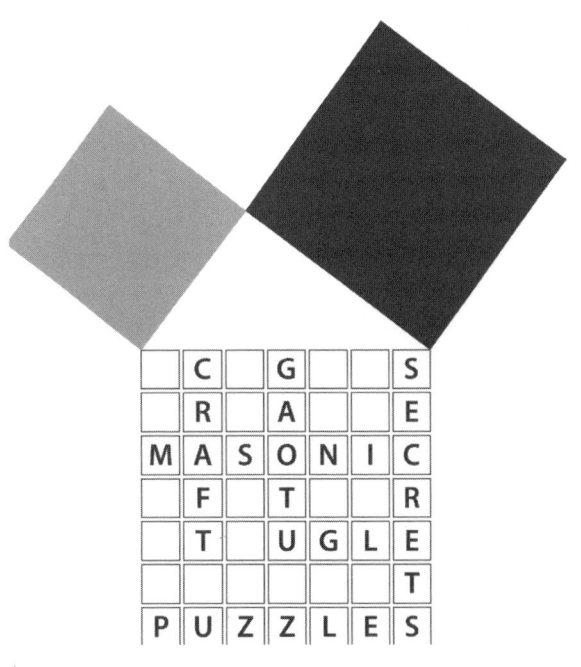

Seb Giroux

First published 2019

ISBN 978 0 85318 570 3

All rights reserved. No part of this book may be reproduced or transmitted in any form or by any means, electronic or mechanical, including photocopying, recording, scanning or by any information storage and retrieval system, on the internet or elsewhere, without permission from the Publisher in writing.

© Seb Giroux 2019

Published by Lewis Masonic

an imprint of Ian Allan Publishing Ltd, Shepperton, Middx TW17 8AS.
Printed in England.

Visit the Lewis Masonic website at www.lewismasonic.co.uk

Copyright

Illegal copying and selling of publications deprives authors, publishers and booksellers of income, without which there would be no investment in new publications. Unauthorised versions of publications are also likely to be inferior in quality and contain incorrect information. You can help by reporting copyright infringements and acts of piracy to the Publisher or the UK Copyright Service.

Picture Credits

Every effort has been made to identify and correctly attribute photographic credits. Should any error have occurred this is entirely unintentional.

A brief introduction to Freemasonry

Freemasonry. The word conjures up dozens of conspiracy theories from hidden treasures to a shadowy global government. Undoubtedly, a society so full of secrets must have evil intentions...

The truth is, there really aren't that many secrets. Some words, some gestures are kept hidden from non-members, but most of what we do is out in the open. Ceremonies take place behind closed doors, but the content of our rituals, with the exception of a few words, is very much available for all to read.

Freemasonry has permeated our world for centuries, and quite often, in a very constructive manner (pun intended). The symbols and traditions bear strong meaning not just for the Brothers who repeat them during the ceremonies, but for every one. Through commercial exploitation, some of the symbolism may have been corrupted, but there is nothing nefarious about any of it.

By their nature, symbols can be interpreted in many ways and therefore caution should always be exercised against the temptation to see things that are not really there.

Various buildings in our cities and many expressions commonly used have a Masonic origin. Many great historical figures were members of the Fraternity. People like B. Franklin, P. Revere or G. Washington for instance.

Should you wish to reflect on what they brought from Freemasonry into the creation of the United States, you may choose to focus on social concepts such as equality and fraternity. These were far more essential in shaping their new country than the presumed symbolism one may see on the map of the U.S capital city or on the one dollar bill.

So then, what is Freemasonry? Every brother learns at some point that Freemasonry is a *"peculiar system of morality veiled in allegories and illustrated by symbols"*. A bit of a mouthful, but remember this was written centuries ago.

The word *peculiar* in this context means unique rather than odd. The *system of morality* is compatible with any faiths and beliefs and does not take over, replace or impose any specific ones.

Symbols and allegories are used essentially to teach valuable lessons of morality to the brethren and bring the rituals to life. As ever, context is everything.

Beyond this definition, Freemasonry is merely a social club that blends charity and theatre. It does impose strict acceptance criteria, but most associations or clubs do. The social side of Freemasonry is what binds people together who would otherwise never have met. It is the glue of the Order.

Developing one's sense of morality is at the heart of Freemasonry. But it doesn't make it a religion. Freemasonry does not impose its own deity, doesn't offer a promise of salvation and doesn't demand a particular faith, but rather a general belief in a Supreme Being. It promotes equality among Brothers and within the Lodge, dismisses all external differences, be they social, professional or otherwise. The only accepted distinctions are that of office and rank within the Lodge itself. In this sense, Freemasonry was incredibly progressive in the 17th century.

Let's briefly address gender equality. Women have been allowed in Freemasonry for well over a hundred years in either women only or mixed Lodges. There are also mixed gender Orders such as the Eastern Star. However, it is true to say that Freemasonry still carries the old tradition of stonecutters lodges which were only open to men. This remains the current position, but it might evolve in the future.

As a final word, Freemasons are indeed free. Free to join and leave as they wish. Free to join several Lodges and mingle with many brothers. Free to rise through the ranks and take on increasing responsibilities to ensure a smooth running of the Fraternity. Free to apply to any Appendant Order as long as they meet the entry criteria. Free to do as little in the Lodge as they wish, or be involved in every part of its administration. Free to enjoy themselves, make friends, and if I may just add: free to laugh out loud every time a ludicrous conspiracy theory comes to light.

But you really do not have to believe me on that last one.

Learning and development is an important element of Freemasonry.

Freemasonry Today No. 43 - September 2018

    R.W. Bro. Sir David Wootton
    Assistant Grand Master

We need to find something that communicates the unique nature of Freemasonry in a friendly and accessible fashion, and in a way which makes us an attractive use of our potential members' precious time.

Caretakers, Risk-Takers and Undertakers: the Three Faces of UGLE Quarterly Commnication - 12th day of December 2018

    V.W. Bro. Dr. D.R. Staples
    Grand Secretary
    C.E.O of the United Grand Lodge of England

For the Freemasons

This book will contribute to your daily advancement in a very pleasant way.

Inside, you will find games, puzzles, questions to challenge your existing knowledge and possibly add to it.

You can of course go through the 100 puzzles on your own. But you can also share them with others in the Lodge.

Here's a few ideas of how you can use the book:

- Ask a few questions during a meeting, for instance while waiting for the candidate to be prepared.
- Share some interesting facts with the brethren during LoI.
- Help dispel myths about the Order with your family and friends.
- Run a quiz during the Festive Board, make it a charity game.
- As a mentor, propose some games to candidates, EAs or FCs while they are waiting outside.
- Generate discussions during a lodge dinner.
- Inspire prospective candidates with a pub quiz.

These are just a few ideas, you are welcome to make up your own way of using the puzzles contained therein to help promote Freemasonry and debunk the myths.

No matter where you are on your Masonic journey, I hope you can enjoy a little bit of lighthearted and casual time whilst potentially learning something new about the Order.

The utmost care has been applied in compiling the book to respect our Landmarks and avoid any mistakes. Should you spot something you believe is not quite accurate, please let us know and we will endeavour to correct.

For the general public

It is said that Freemasonry comes from time immemorial, that it is the oldest, broadest, best known fraternity in the world and above all, that it is not a secret society but a society with secrets. But is this all true?

The mere word Freemasonry is enough to conjure up all kind of wild speculations and conspiracy theories. Countless books, movies, dramas have featured the Order. From figuring on iconic buildings to allowing a rewrite of History, Masonic symbols have been used in every possible manner the human imagination can conceive.

Are secrets truly hidden in plain sight, for all to see?

Time to separate facts from fibs.
Time to promote the truth in a fun and enjoyable fashion.

With all its assorted games, this book is bound to keep you entertained for hours on end. The questions are varied and cover a wide range of topics from history to symbolism and from famous Masons to the rituals.
And yes, we will also talk about the secrets...

So, come on in!

Freemasonry is open to anyone. We really are a nice bunch, you'll see. Resolve these riveting puzzles, answer the intriguing questions, find out about famous Masons of the past, discover compelling quirky facts, debunk some of the preposterous myths, chuckle at the jokes and impress your friends with your newly aquired Masonic knowledge.

All the facts used throughout the puzzles and quiz as well as in the answers are accurate and verifiable.

Where any doubt exists in the general and current knowledge of the Order, the author mentions it clearly.

Source and Bibliography

Various books and websites have been used in the creation of the puzzles, and in the validation of the answers. You can find some listed below.

Web
The website of the United Grand Lodge of England (UGLE)
https://www.ugle.org.uk/

Solomon, online resource from UGLE to learn more about Freemasonry
https://solomon.ugle.org.uk/

The Library and Museum of Freemasonry, London
https://museumfreemasonry.org.uk/

Scottish Rite - The Supreme Council, 33º, SJ, USA
https://scottishrite.org/

Quatuor Coronati Correspondence Circle
https://www.quatuorcoronati.com/
(*plus their regular publications - also available at Lewis Publishing*)

Books
Gan, R. - *Secret Handshakes and Rolled-up Trouser Legs: The Secrets of Freemasonry.* Ian Allan Publishing Ltd
Gest, K.L. - *Freemasonry Decoded.* Ian Allan Publishing Ltd,
Harrison, D. - A quick Guide to *Freemasonry.* Ian Allan Publishing Ltd,
Mackey, A. - *An Encyclopædia of Freemasonry and Its Kindred Sciences.* L.H. Evans & Co
Moore, D. - *A Guide to Masonic Symbolism.* Ian Allan Publishing Ltd,
Waite, A.E. - *A New Encyclopaedia of Freemasonry.* Wings Books

About the Author

A French native, I moved to the U.K. over 16 years ago. A few years back, a good friend of mine invited me to join Freemasonry and I was initiated in December 2014.

The brothers present during my interview seem to remember very well one particular answer I gave. They told me that books were not allowed during the ceremonies and therefore there was a lot of learning to be done. Then, they asked if I had a good memory.
"Well, I have learned another language, haven't I?"

My masonic journey has only just started. At the time of compiling this first puzzle book, I am Junior Warden in my mother Lodge. My apron is a lovely pale blue. This shows that every Freemason can contribute one way or another.

In my few years on the Square, I have very much enjoyed discovering new symbols, their origins, their moral meanings and how they can relate to my every day life. I have devoured various books and documents, especially on the origins of the Order. Today, I am delighted to be given such an opportunity to share my knowledge in a stimulatingly different form.

I passionately believe that Freemasonry should be first and foremost fun and entertaining. Brothers should very much enjoy their journey, however far they want to take it, and wherever it leads them.

I wish you a fantastic time with these puzzles and quiz. Enjoy learning a thing or two about Freemasonry and maybe even impress your friends with some surprising trivia.

I bid you farewell, and hope to meet you on the Level soon.

How to use the book

The book includes 100 questions, quiz, puzzles and games divided into the following six categories:

Puzzles
Games such as crossword, word search, maze, cryptic messages and so on.

Debunk the myths
Challenge your perception and your beliefs with these questions.

Spot the Mason
Identify a famous Freemason.

Pub quiz
Multiple choice questions. Pick the right answer to win, but be careful that sometimes more than one may be correct.

Did you know?
Interesting, peculiar or unexpected Masonic fact

Are you worthy?
Masonic questions that only the most worthy of all will be able to answer! You have been warned.

Mark 1 point for each correct answer or when you complete a game.

In addition, the book contains a treasure quest. It begins with puzzle 3. All the answers within the quest are numbers which gives you the next question. The quest leads you to an ultimate challenge where you might win additional points.

To best enjoy the quest, start with puzzle 3 before attempting any other puzzle or quiz in this book. See if you can navigate all the way until you find the hidden treasure!

Finally, a little hint: ˙˙˙sǝɯᴉʇ ʇɐ dlǝɥ ʇɥbᴉɯ ʇᴉ 'ʍouʞ ɹǝʌǝu no⅄
　　　　　　　　　　　　　˙ʞooq sᴉɥʇ oʇ uoᴉʇɔnpoɹʇuᴉ ǝɥʇ pɐǝɹ oʇ ǝɯoɔlǝʍ ǝɹɐ no⅄

The Mysteries of Freemasonry

 **Puzzle 1**

The size of King Solomon's Temple is recorded in a historic unit called cubit. For instance, the two pillars placed in its porchway entrance were 17.5 cubits high.

What is a cubit?

 Puzzle 2

During the medieval time of operative masonry, masons could often be found in a lodge. What was a lodge back then?

A. A location near a building site where the architect lived.

B. The school where apprentices learned their skills.

C. A temporary workshop set alongside the building in construction where stones would be prepared.

D. A secret place where they would hold private meetings.

Puzzle 3

The quest starts here

When did it all start?

The answer is a specific year.
Use the second half to find the next question of the quest.

Find solutions page 54

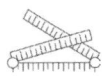

Puzzle 4 - Purple Paragraph

The text below discusses allegories and symbolism in Freemasonry. Sadly, however, the punctuation and spaces have all been forgotten, and some letters have been erased.

Can you recompose the text?

MAN · OFTHESY · BOLSUS · DINFRE · MASONR ·
FIND · HEIRORI · ININ · EDIEVA · OPE · ATIV
ESTONE · ASONR · ATA · IMEWH · NLITE · ACYW
A · STILLVE · YRARET · ACHING · ASMOSTL · D
O · EVIASY · BOLS · NDALLE · ORIESANALLEG
ORYISASTORYTHATCANCONVEYMORALMEAN
INGSLIKEAMET · PHO · FREE · ASONRYISVEI
L · DINA · LEGORI · SWHI · HMEA · STHAT · OUG
ET · OSEEMOR · SYMBO · SANDU · DERSTANDT ·
EALLEGOR · ESB · TTERASY · UPROG · ESSTHR
· UGHT · EDEGREESI · THIS · ENSEFREE · ASO
NRY · EQUIRESCA · DIDATES · OBEPA · IENTA
· DKEEN · ODEVELO · T · EIROWNK · OWLED · EA
NDS · NSEOFM · RALIT ·

Puzzle 5

How is the son of a Freemason called?

Hint: *This name is close to my publisher's heart...*

Find solutions page 54

The Mysteries of Freemasonry 3

 **Puzzle 6**

In the past, the Freemasons have used a particular type of secret code sometimes referred to as the Masonic Cypher. In France, it has also been used by Napoleon. In the United States, during the American Civil War, it was employed by Union prisoners to communicate among themselves.

What is the usual name of this cypher?

Hint: *Imagine the dots are farm animals and the grid represents their house...*

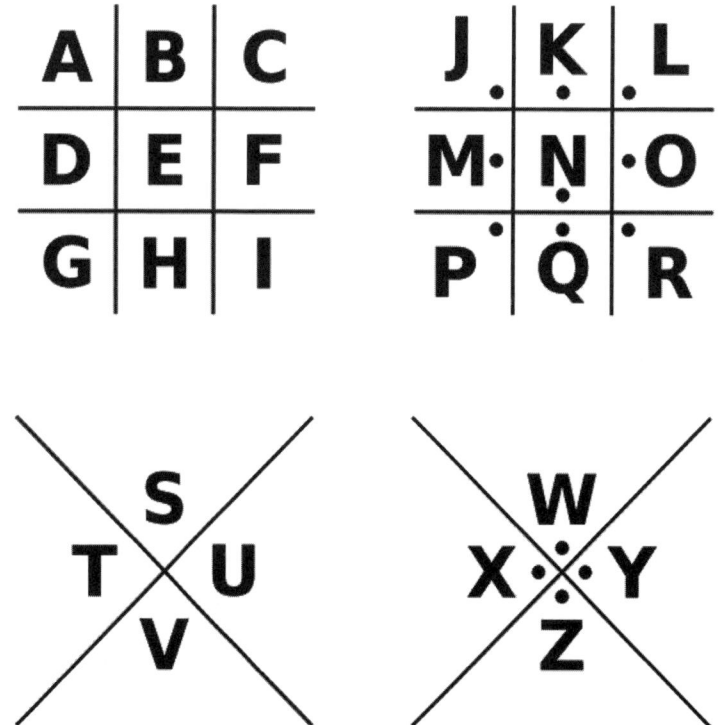

Find solutions page 54

Puzzle 7

What is my job?

> In Freemasonry, I am the bouncer: I keep the door shut when a meeting is in progress and make sure nobody gets in unless they can prove to me they are worthy. It is my duty to prepare the candidates before their ceremonies. In regular Freemasonry, I am the only brother allowed to carry a sword, it makes me look scary at time. My office in the Lodge is one that can attract remuneration.

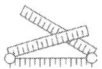 **Puzzle 8 - Code and cypher**

Someone has sent a personal message, but it is encrypted.

> Using the Masonic Cypher discovered earlier in puzzle 6, can you decode the hidden message?

Here are some example of the code:

⌡ = A   ╱╲ = V   ⌊.⌋ = K

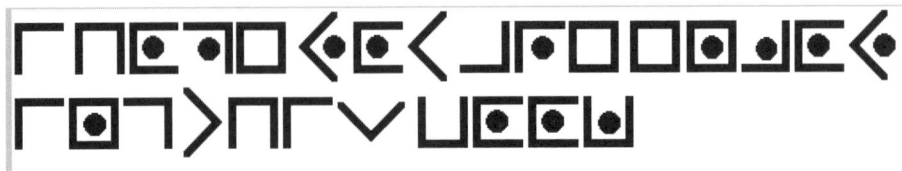

Find solutions page 54-55

The Mysteries of Freemasonry 5

 Puzzle 9

Which of these are considered to be **"Truly Masonic Ornaments"** by every Freemasons?

    A. Power and Persuasion
    B. Benevolence and Charity
    C. Secrets and Brotherhood

 Puzzle 10

Why do freemasons wear white gloves?

 **Puzzle 11**

What am I?

> Built in Jerusalem under the reign of a very famous king, it is thought that I was the first of my kind. My design may have been inspired by the Phoenicians, although, since no blueprint subsists today, nobody knows what I really looked like. It is believed that I hosted the Ark of the Covenant. I stood firmly for over four centuries before being destroyed by the Babylonians in 586 BCE.
>
> I am at the centre of Freemasonic traditional history and am the source of many symbols.

Find solutions page 55

Puzzle 12 - Word search

A few Masonic words have been lost in the grid below.

Can you find them?

```
P E D E S T A L N B G D R D Q Q B Q B P
K Z I O T H G L O V E S L T F L A A M D
Q S G D O O H R E H T O R B O A P S S R
F N E R I N J C F C N U P C P N P H B A
T R Y W A Y V B W O O Y A H U D R L Q O
L L E H X N L E A M I D I A N M E A R B
E N A G J G D V C P T X Y R O A N R I E
R A K Y A L Q M N A U D G I R R T A T V
A K N M U L O C A S T P V T P K I Y A I
L E V F T M I H B S I X I Y A S C N Y T
U G J U F H A A E E T C M E Y S E F W S
C D Z Y A A G V N S S E Y E X O I H V E
I O C I R N M D E H N S R R C L G L Q F
D L X Y C D S X V L O Q X G S O E S N C
N N X Q W S N Y O X C U L E S M F M R N
E R L Q O H H B L A R A A D G O W A G R
P S M Z L A I O E H S R U J N N F A P J
R H O O L K R J N Q F E T F Q T O G D L
E C H N E E A M C N P M I B N I G W B E
P M B U F R M F E C Q P R F J C G F W K
```

APPRENTICE	CRAFT	LODGE
APRON	DEGREE	PEDESTAL
ASHLAR	FELLOWCRAFT	PERPENDICULAR
BENEVOLENCE	FESTIVEBOARD	REGALIA
BROTHERHOOD	GLOVES	RITUAL
CHARITY	GRANDMASTER	SOLOMON
COLUMN	HANDSHAKE	SQUARE
COMPASSES	HIRAM	
CONSTITUTION	LANDMARKS	

Find solutions page 55

The Mysteries of Freemasonry 7

 Puzzle 13

What is the usual length (in inches) of the gauge used by a Freemason?

The answer gives you the next question of the quest.

Hint: *What in a day...*

 Puzzle 14

Freemasonry is well known for having secrets.

But what do these secrets consist of exactly, what is their nature?

Find solutions page 55

Puzzle 15

Which of these musicians was Freemason? (*multiple answers possible*)

  A. Beethoven
  B. Mozart
  C. Liszt
  D. Haydn
  E. Sibelius

    Puzzle 16

Which of the following was inspired by Masonic symbols?

A.

C.

B.

D.

The Facebook logo is registered trademarks of Facebook, Inc.
Google and the Google and Gmail logos are registered trademarks of Google LLC
Used with permission.

Find solutions page 55

The Mysteries of Freemasonry

 **Puzzle 17**

At what age can one become a Freemason?

Use the answer to follow the quest.

 Puzzle 18

The word Master is used in a variety of contexts by Freemasons. Can you correct the following sentences by placing the bold words in the right sentence?

A. Hiram Abiff, who is called our **Worshipful Master** by all Freemasons, was the Chief Architect of Solomon's Temple.

B. The **Master Mason** of the Lodge is installed every year to rule the Lodge.

C. Every brother who has taken his third degree is entitled to be called a **Master**.

 Puzzle 19

What am I?

I originate in Greek mythology where it is said that after baby Zeus broke the horn off a goat, his nurse filled it with an inexhaustible supply of food or drinks. I am often depicted as a spiral-shaped basket laden with fruits.
For Freemasons, I am the symbol of plenitude.

Puzzle 20

Can you match the regalia below to the appropriate brother?

A. Fellowcraft

B. Royal Arch Companion

C. Craft Grand Officer

D. Mark Mason Master

E. Rose Croix (18th Degree)

F. Knight Templar

G. Craft Worshipful Master

 **Puzzle 21**

What is the highest degree of the Scottish Rite?

The answer gives you the next question of the quest.

Find solutions page 56-57

The Mysteries of Freemasonry   11

 Puzzle 22

Which of these flowers is often associated with Freemasonry?

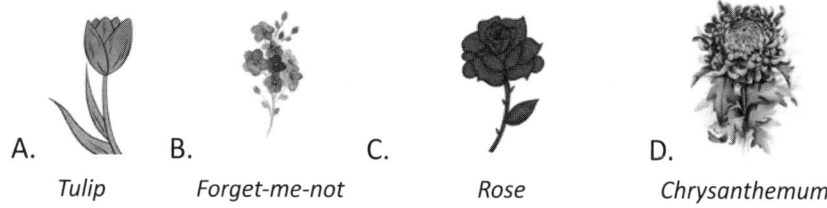

A. Tulip   B. Forget-me-not   C. Rose   D. Chrysanthemum

 **Puzzle 23**

After becoming a Master Mason (Third Degree), a brother may wish to further his Masonic career. Two main Rites are available to him, can you name them?

Hint: *sǝɯɐu lɐɔᴉɥdɐɹƃoǝƃ ʇnoqɐ ʞuᴉɥꞱ*

 Puzzle 24

In the Book of Constitutions, there is a specific rule that asks the Worshipful Master to display the warrant of the Lodge at the beginning of every meeting to demonstrate the authority under which the Lodge operates. What is the number associated to this rule?

Use the answer to follow the quest.

Find solutions page 57

 ## Puzzle 25 - Charade

My first is not low.

My second is to sheep what a man is to people.

My third leads the 26 but is pronounced like a surprise.

When my fourth is alive, it has a different name than when we eat it.

My whole lived centuries ago and lies at the heart of Freemasonry's Traditional History.

 ## Puzzle 26

When a brother is installed as the Master of the Lodge, it is said that he now occupies the _____ of _____.

Hint: *Think about furniture*

 ## Puzzle 27

Washington D.C. was created towards the end of the 18th century. When they agreed the design and layout, did the U.S. forefathers drew giant Masonic symbols throughout the streets of their capital city?

 ## Puzzle 28

Who are the "**sons of a widow**"?

Find solutions page 57-58

The Mysteries of Freemasonry   13

     Puzzle 29

Which part of your car was invented by a Freemason?

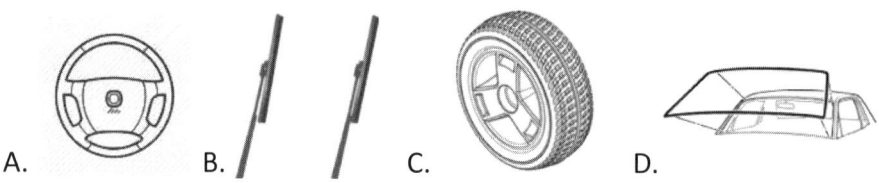

     Puzzle 30

How is the Third Degree ceremony also called?

     Puzzle 31

Who am I?

> The son of a farmer, I was born in Ayrshire in 1881. At the age of 13, I moved to London to train as a doctor. In 1906, I worked at St Mary's Hospital Medical School. It is there that a mistake attracted my attention. A set of dishes that had been used previously to grow the staphylococci germ started to react to the influenza virus in a strange manner. By analysing this phenomenon further, I went on to make a discovery that would change medical science and save countless lives worldwide.
> For this work, I earned the Nobel Prize in medicine.

Find solutions page 58

 **Puzzle 32**

If operative masons were those skilled individuals who actually carved the stones for building purposes, then by contrast, how do we call a modern Freemason who doesn't cut stones at all? He is a _____ **Mason**

 Puzzle 33

Which Euclid proposition is very close to a freemason's heart?

The answer gives you the next question of the quest.

Hint: *Pythagoras knew this*

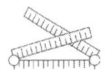 **Puzzle 34 - Logic Game**

Five Brothers meet during a Masonic event. They are allowed to wear their chosen regalia. They talk about their role in their mother Lodge and also about their work outside Freemasonry.

After being served their favourite drink, they stand next to each other in a line for a group photo.

Using the clues next page, **can you find out who the journalist is and where he comes from**?

Find solutions page 59

The Mysteries of Freemasonry

Background information

- The five brothers are meeting in London for a UGLE meeting.
- They all come from a different Province.
- Each brother wears an apron of a specific colour.
- These 5 brothers all have their own drink.
- They hold a different office in their respective mother Lodge.
- They also all come from a diverse professional background.

Below is what we know already about these brothers. They are standing side by side in front of the photographer.

1. The wearer of a pink apron comes from North Wales.
2. The wearer of a beige apron is a barrister.
3. The wearer of a red apron drinks orange juice.
4. The brother from Northumberland stands on the left of the one from Suffolk.
5. The brother who is secretary in his Lodge is a bricklayer by trade.
6. The brother from London is Junior Warden in his Lodge.
7. The brother in the centre of the group drinks coffee.
8. The light blue apron is the first on the left of the photo.
9. The brother who is Senior Deacon stands next to the Police officer.
10. The teacher stands next to the brother Junior Warden.
11. The brother who has no office in his lodge drinks red wine.
12. The brother in dark blue apron is a mentor.
13. The brother with the light blue apron is next to the brother from Wiltshire.
14. The brother from Northumberland prefers to drink Tea.
15. The brother who is Senior Deacon stands next to the brother who drinks Prosecco.

You now hold all the information you need to identify the Journalist.

*For some added fun, feel free to use a timer
and see if you can resolve this puzzle in 20 minutes or less!*

Find solutions page 59

Puzzle 35

Who am I?

> Known by some as Black Jack, I was born in Missouri (U.S.) in 1860. In 1882, I was sworn a West Point cadet. I returned to the Academy in 1897 as an instructor. My rigidity made me quite unpopular with the cadets and got me the derogatory surname of Black Jack. In 1905, and with the approval of Congres, president Roosevelt appointed me General. When the United States entered the conflict in Europe in May 1917, I was selected by President Wilson to take command of the American army. In 1919, a new rank was created for me and I became the General of the Armies of the United States, the highest possible rank. I retired from service in 1924 and died in 1948.

 **Puzzle 36**

How does one get to wear a light blue apron for the first time?

 Puzzle 37

Was Leonardo Da Vinci a Freemason?

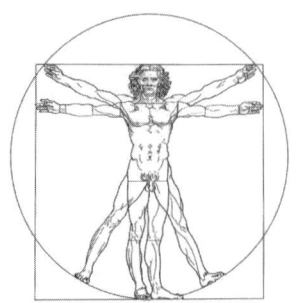

Find solutions page 60

The Mysteries of Freemasonry 17

 Puzzle 38

Is this summary True or False?

There is an intimate and historical connection between the Knights Templar and the Freemasons.

After the demise of their Order on October 13, 1307 (a Friday), most of the surviving Knights Templar moved to Scotland where they remained hidden for a considerable time.

Over a century later, their descendants and heirs started to regroup. During their secret meetings, they developed rituals and ceremonies that nowadays form part of what is known as the Scottish Rite. Throughout the 16th century, this reborn Templar movement started spreading across England. There, in the late 17th century, they opened some of the first Freemasonic Lodges.

By 1717 however, Freemasonry had grown as a separate order, and they decided to split from the Knights Templar. Freemasonry grew to public prominence while the Knights Templar preferred to remain in the shadow.

Today, they are very separate, but they share a prestigious history.

 Puzzle 39

What expression of Masonic origin can you use to present someone who is honest and truthful?

Find solutions page 60

Puzzle 40 - Crossword of the Entered Apprentice

Find out the hidden word on row 6 (Hotizontal 13)

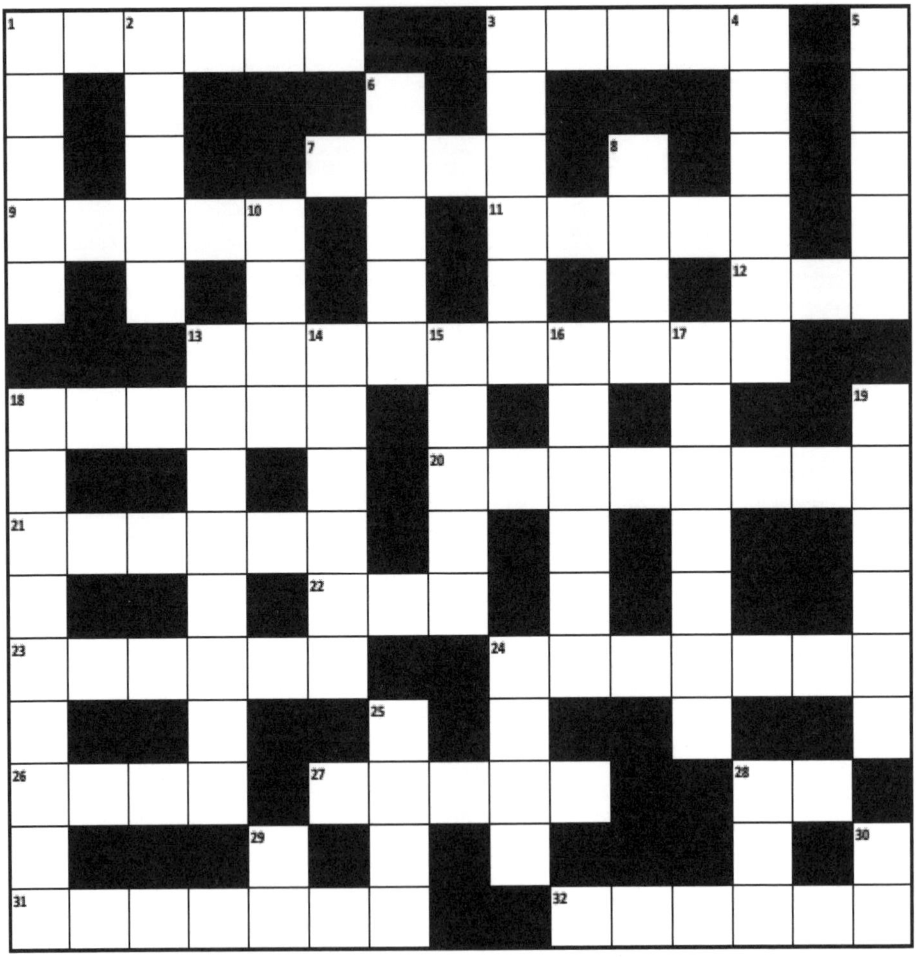

Find solutions page 60

The Mysteries of Freemasonry

Horizontal

1. Upright, cylindrical, supporting.
3. Architectural style recognisable by a thick square abacus resting on a rounded moulding.
7. A particular space, often dedicated for a specific use.
9. Strong belief, spiritual conviction.
11. A common item of furniture in the temple or the office.
12. The Almighty.
18. Forms an angle in buildings.
20. Found above the doors of cathedrals.
21. Sums of what can be found in a wallet.
22. Wander aimlessly
23. Has made amend.
24. Joyful time after a Lodge meeting.
26. Male descendants.
27. "Bouncer" outside the Lodge.
28. Most likely to be elected Worshipful Master (abr.)
31. Famous King from ancient times
32. Became a member, linked

Vertical

1. Require skills.
2. Can help you lift heavy objects.
3. Works the floor of the Lodge.
4. Lecture given to the candidate after his initiation.
5. Some are used to chop.
6. Opposite to Chaos.
8. Three of them together brought presents fit for a king.
10. Only the optimist has it.
13. From a long time ago.
14. Of immense value (British spelling).
15. What you might be told as you are allowed in.
16. Where Jesus expelled merchants.
17. Helps those in needs.
18. Used for drawing circles.
19. Symbolic and distinctive badge.
24. Unattached.
25. A type of song mostly used to praise.
28. Shine high in the sky.
29. He used to rule the Lodge.
30. Walks the candidate on his initiation.

Find solutions page 60

Puzzle 41

Who am I?

My family already had a long connection with Freemasonry when I was initiated in 1901. Due to other commitments, I resigned from my Lodge in 1912 but continued to contribute to Freemasonry throughout my life. Although born an English man, I was made an honorary citizen of the United States in 1963 for my decisive actions during WWII. I was made a Knight of the Garter, received the Order of Merit and also the Nobel Prize in Literature. I spent most of my life in British politics. The Russians compared me to a bulldog and that image has been associated with me ever since.

 ## Puzzle 42

By what other name is Freemasonry sometimes called by the Freemasons?

Hint: *Remember Freemasonry evolved from medieval stone cutters*

 ## Puzzle 43

If you ever had to pick a firearm, which Masonic inventor could help you?

A. Beretta
B. Colt
C. Glock

D. Smith
E. Wesson
F. Kalashnikov

Find solutions page 60-61

The Mysteries of Freemasonry

Puzzle 44

Freemasonry is organised in several Grand Lodges. Most countries are covered by a single Grand Lodge although there can be more. For instance, in the United States where many states have their own Grand Lodge.

Is there an overall organisation that governs all Grand lodges within Freemasonry and if so, what is it called?

Puzzle 45

Why are Freemasons called "**free**"?

Puzzle 46

Freemasonry is known for using a multitude of symbols.

    What is their purpose?

Puzzle 47

London was once home to two rival Grand Lodges. In the early 19th century, two brothers decided that a truce was necessary for the better good of Freemasonry. Each was the Grand Master of one of the Grand Lodges. The younger brother bowed to his elder, and the rival Lodges of England were finally united. In what year did that take place? 18xx

xx gives you the next question of the quest

Find solutions page 61

Puzzle 48 - Cluedo

Can you find the culprit before any other player?

For once the rumours have been right: something terrible has happened in the Lodge! A poor candidate has been assassinated. The Lodge being closed during the ceremony, it is clear that one of the brothers did it. But who? Where in the Lodge? And also, what object did they use to commit this awful crime? Nobody wants to say a word.

A team of four police inspectors have been sent to investigate. You are one of them, and this time you will beat them all and find the answer first.

After interrogation, you have all agreed that only 6 individuals could have done it.

There are also only 6 possible objects and 6 possible locations.
They are summarised in 3 sets of cards below.

Suspect	Location	Object
Master	Entrance	Square
Senior Warden	North East Corner	Compasses
Junior Warden	North	Level
Senior Deacon	South	Plumb Rule
Junior Deacon	West	Wand
Inner Guard	East	Gavel

Each inspector holds 3 cards randomly selected, one from each set.

You can only see yours.

These are your three cards:

Senior Deacon – North – Wand

Find solutions page 61

The Mysteries of Freemasonry 23

The rules are:
- It is assumed that you can reach any location in the Lodge.
- If a player (including yourself) holds a card, they must show it.
- If a player holds 2 cards, they can decide to show only 1 or both.
- You are allowed to call any of the cards you hold.
- You are allowed to propose a solution right after your turn.
- The winner is the first to call out the three correct elements (suspect, location, object).

The interrogation of witnesses have been conducted for some time. The transcript reads like this:

Round 1

Inspector 1 asks for	SD	Compass	Entrance
Card presented by	You	Insp. 2	Insp. 4
Inspector 2 asks for	SW	Square	NE Corner
Card presented by	Insp. 4	Insp. 3	-
You ask for	Master	Wand	South
Card presented by	Insp. 1	-	-
Inspector 3 asks for	JW	Level	East
Card presented by	Insp. 2	Insp. 1	-
Inspector 4 asks for	IG	Gavel	West
Card presented by	-	-	Insp. 3

Round 2

Inspector 1 asks for	JD	Plumb rule	North
Card presented by	-	Insp. 4	You
Inspector 2 asks for	IG	Gavel	South
Card presented by	Insp. 3	-	Insp. 1
You ask for	JD	Wand	NE Corner
Card presented by	-	-	Insp. 2

You now boldly claim to have the solution – what is it?

Find solutions page 61

Puzzle 49

Was Mozart a Freemason?

 Puzzle 50

Who or what is the Quatuor Coronati?

 **Puzzle 51**

What happens when someone is made a "**Mason at sight**"?

 Puzzle 52

It is well known that a candidate for Freemasonry must roll up one of his trouser legs for the initiation ceremony.

But why is that?

Find solutions page 61-62

The Mysteries of Freemasonry   25

 **Puzzle 53**

What am I?

Established in 1850, it took 23 years for Freemasonry to accept me as an Appendant body. My headquarters are based near Washington D.C. My charitable foundation has contributed to causes such as Alzheimer, diabetes and asthma research. I exist in over 20 countries and represent more than half a million members. I am open to both men and women and am co-lead by a matron and a patron.

 **Puzzle 54**

Below are the posters of four movies and TV series. They all share a connection with Freemasonry and UGLE in particular.

Do you know what that link is?

Find solutions page 62

Puzzle 55 - Crossword of the Fellowcraft

Can you spot the seven liberal arts and sciences?

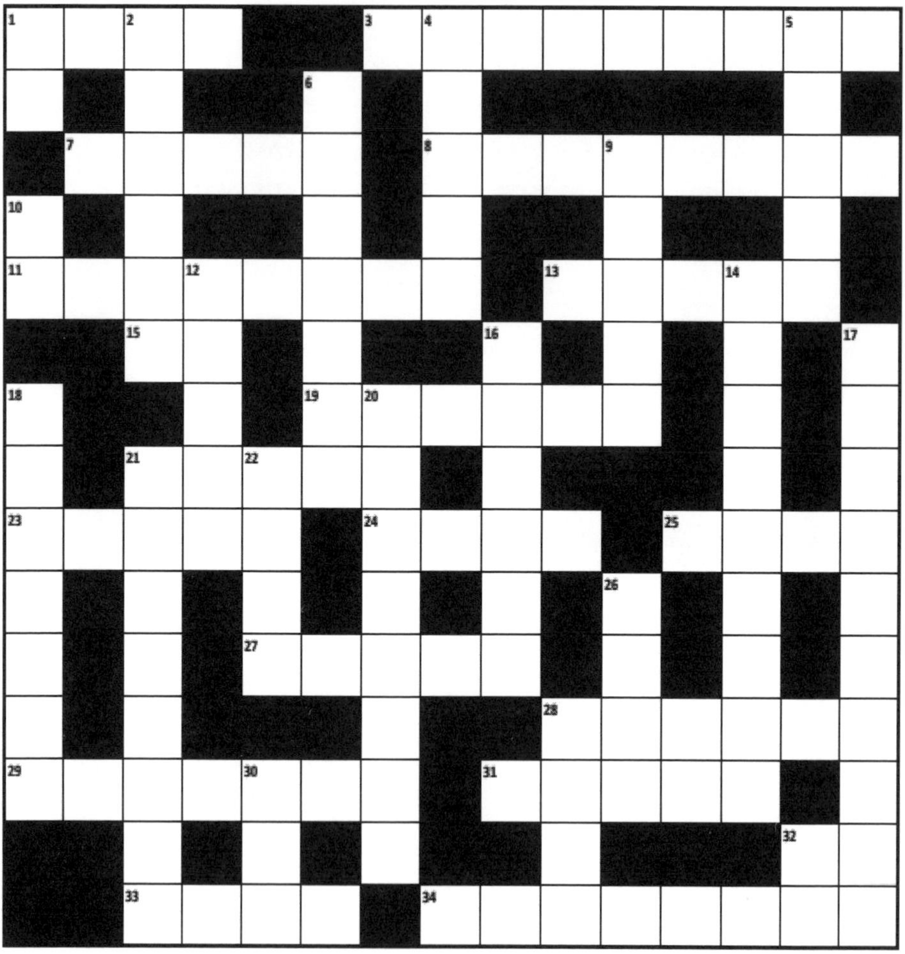

Find solutions page 62-63

The Mysteries of Freemasonry

Horizontal

1. Both exact and morally right.
3. For those who like to gaze at the stars.
7. A delight to the ears.
8. Concerns points, lines, shapes.
11. All there ever was, originally.
13. An attempt.
15. For English.
19. Protection placed over you.
21. Some use spirit or a bubble.
23. Lady justice holds some.
24. Either the first place in a contest or heavy metal.
25. This table is full of them.
27. Makes sense, doesn't it?
28. That which goes around the centre.
29. Language follows its rules.
31. From elbow to finger tip.
32. If it had an "e" at the end, you'd eat it.
33. He rules.
34. Facilitates eloquent delivery.

Vertical

1. First office to carry a wand.
2. In town, you can meet there. In the Lodge, you can meet on it.
4. They indicate/show things.
5. Knows right from wrong.
6. Study it, and you will know.
9. Makes for softer sentences.
10. The one after Vertical 1.
12. Get lower and show submission.
14. He draws it all, even builds it.
16. Forms a pattern, like on the floor.
17. Where 1+1=2.
18. Gives you the Second.
20. Hidden truths hide behind that one.
21. Of great importance, couldn't miss it on a map.
22. That which helps conceal what's in Vertical 20.
26. So mote it be.
28. Full-bodied square.
30. Must be one to enter according to UGLE.
32. All circles share its value.

Find solutions page 62-63

Puzzle 56

Can a Freemason be blackballed?

Puzzle 57

The administrative unit of Freemasonry is the Lodge.

> What is the equivalent within the Holy Royal Arch?

Puzzle 58

Aside from the Lodge, Freemasons like to meet regularly during what they call the LoI.

> What is a LoI?

Find solutions page 63

The Mysteries of Freemasonry

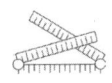

Puzzle 59 - 3D Cube mixup

The Secretary of your Lodge has placed an order for a set of large cubes showcasing some Masonic jewels. Sadly, the original template was lost and the manufacturer sent four different samples. The symbols seem to have been printed randomly. Only one of the cubes is correct.

By luck, the Worshipful Master has managed to recover an early draft of the template. He must now find out which of the four samples below is the correct one.

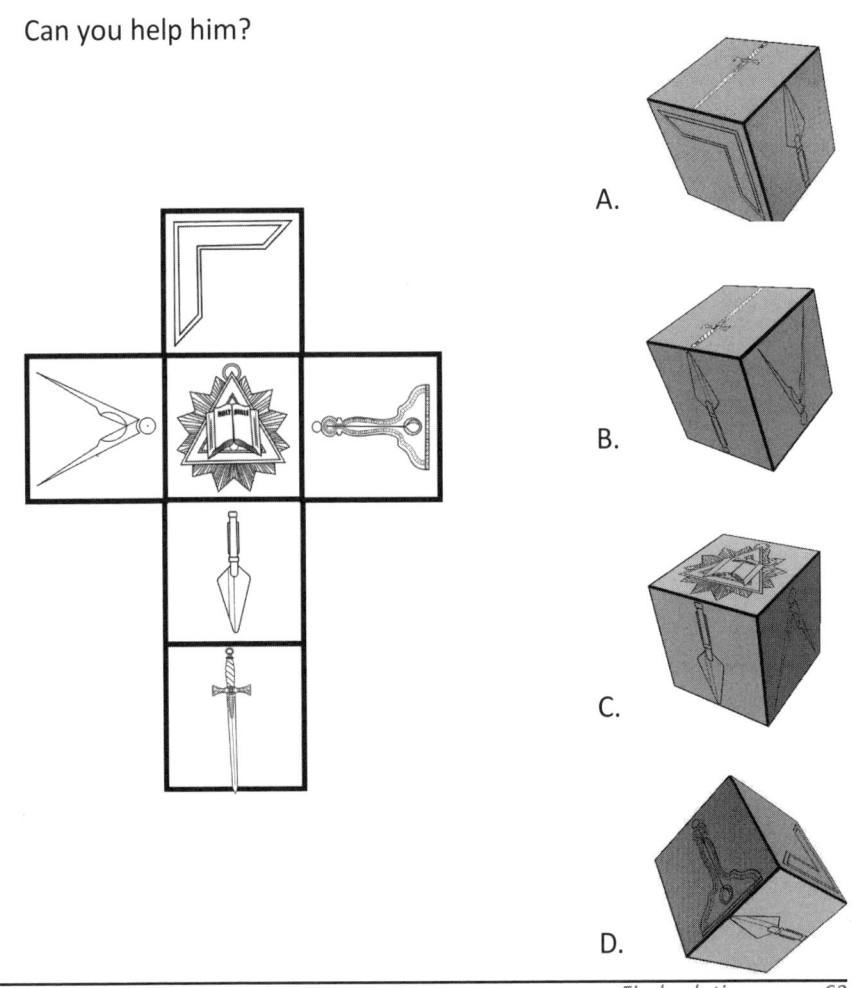

Can you help him?

A.

B.

C.

D.

Find solutions page 63

30

Puzzle 60

According to the Bible, what are the names of the 2 pillars that stood on the porch of Solomon's temple?

Find solutions page 63

The Mysteries of Freemasonry

Puzzle 61

Which of the following fictional sleuth can claim a Masonic origin?

    A. Hercule Poirot   D. Magnum P.I

    B. Sherlock Holmes   E. Columbo

    C. Nancy Drew

Puzzle 62

The Grand lodge in England is called United Grand Lodge of England (UGLE). Why the word "**United**"?

Puzzle 63

How many Presidents of the United States of America were known Freemasons?

As an additional challenge...

    could you name them all?

Find solutions page 63

Puzzle 64

Who am I?

American citizen born in 1930, I spent my career in the Military. Although my father wanted me to join the Naval Academy, I quickly discovered I was seasick and went for the sky instead. Perhaps inspired by my mother's maiden name, I can be said to have gone "further than any other Freemason ever has". In 1969, I joined one of the most exclusive clubs that ever existed. Afterwards, I was awarded the Presidential Medal of Freedom.

Millions of people still associate me with the particular walk I showcased in summer of '69. My first name is not well known because of my sister Fay. When we were kids, she struggled to pronounce the word "brother", and I ended being known as "buzzer" instead. This name has stuck to me ever since.

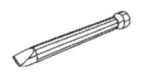

Puzzle 65

Where am I?

A city, now famous and visited by many tourists, I once stood on the North bank of a river, concentrated in only about a square mile. A lot of buildings still standing today were designed and built by Freemasons. Rich of many inns, bars and pubs, it is no surprise that my first Grand Lodge originated in one. After being severely damaged by fire in the 17th Century, I rose again from the ashes, thanks in great part to a brilliant architect who rebuilt me, including a total of 52 churches. Actually, he may have been one of the very first Freemasons, but that would be for another question.

Find solutions page 64

The Mysteries of Freemasonry

Puzzle 66

One Freemason can boast of being among the very few humans to have named a country. Who is he, and what is the country?

Hint: *What is the latin for "Unknown land in the South"?*

Puzzle 67

A candidate must not hold onto any of it as he enters the Lodge for his initiation. If he carries any on him, then the ceremony must be stopped and started all over again.

What is it?

Puzzle 68

Is this statement True or False?

The all-seeing eye on the Great Seal of the United States and the one dollar bill share a common Masonic origin.

Find solutions page 64

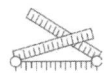

Puzzle 69 - Crossword of the Master Mason

The Motto of Freemasonry is hidden in this grid... can you spot it?

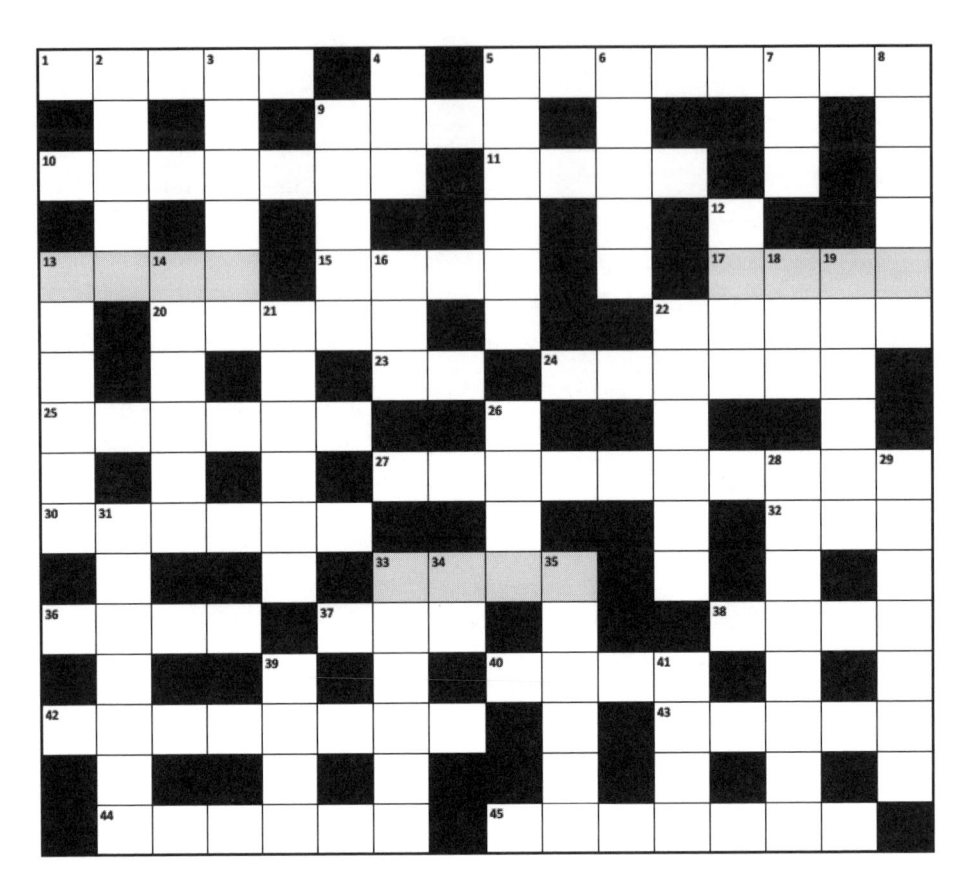

Horizontal

1. Very gothic sort of arch.
5. Degree of power, force.
9. Where is it?
10. To hide meanings within an image, a metaphor.
11. Has, possesses.

Vertical

2. The Highest Master for an EA.
3. One who suffers.
4. Not pristine anymore.
5. Buildings are made of them.
6. Distinguish one's position in an organised society.

Find solutions page 65

The Mysteries of Freemasonry

Horizontal	**Vertical**
15. Old English for conceal.	7. He or Him.
20. Void of much.	8. Mansion above.
22. Wants to eavesdrop on Masonic meetings.	9. First thing ever created.
23. The first step in Freemasonry	12. Most things lie underneath.
24. Unclose, again.	13. Used to mark where to dig.
25. Round and round it goes.	14. When things get scarce.
27. Of immense worth, almost impossible to replace.	16. Allegedly all-seeing.
30. Start rough, become smooth.	18. Utmost respect mixed with wonder and some fear.
32. Latin king.	19. The wind renders it useless.
36. A gesture which has meaning.	21. Provides strong support.
37. To unearth, one must do this.	22. Cylindrical, tall, reliable.
38. Support the flower.	26. He who feels a strong and eager desire for something.
40. ou might walk thus if your leg gets wounded.	28. Several Freemasons together.
42. Senior members of a community chosen to enforce discipline.	29. Perform some inspection.
43. Distinguishing Badge of a Freemason.	31. A Masonic tool pointing the straight line of conduct one may follow.
44. Where Lodges meet.	33. Held by people of high moral standards.
45. The third degree.	34. On the other side of the door from the Tyler.
	35. Cryptic, hard to understand.
	39. Provide assistance.
	41. As an imperative, allows somebody to enter.

Find solutions page 65

Puzzle 70

After a meeting, Freemasons tend to go for a formal dinner together.

What is this dinner called?

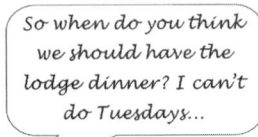

Find solutions page 65

Puzzle 71

Freemasonry uses an allegory of three pillars supporting the Lodge. Each of them represents a great human quality or virtue.

Which of the following are the true Masonic pillars?

A. Honesty – Truth – Justice
B. Wisdom – Strength – Beauty
C. Charity – Benevolence – Care

Puzzle 72

Which two geometrical instruments are placed together, one above the other, to shape the most famous symbol in Freemasonry?

Puzzle 73

What am I?

A block of stone, I am first cut roughly, in the vague shape of a cube. The apprentice starts his carving work before passing me to a more experienced craftsman.
The mason uses a chisel to give me the final shape and render my surface smooth on each side.
In speculative Masonry, I symbolise the progress made by an Entered Apprentice becoming a Fellowcraft and then a Master Mason.

Find solutions page 65

Puzzle 74

Which American car(s) should a Freemason buy?

    A. Ford   C. Cadillac

    B. Chrysler   D. Chevrolet

Puzzle 75

Steve and Paul are both members of the same Lodge. Paul has gone through the chair a while back and Steve was initated last year.

They also happen to work together for a logistics company. Paul is a lorry driver. He rarely meets Steve who, as the director of operations, spends most of his time in the Head Quarters.

When they meet at work, Paul salutes Steve respectfully, acknowledging his senior position within the company.

During a meeting of their Lodge, what is their relationship and how do they salute each other?

Puzzle 76

Three officers rule the Lodge.

    Can you name them?

Find solutions page 65-66

The Mysteries of Freemasonry

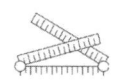

Puzzle 77 - Maze

The path to initiation can be treacherous.

Can you guide the new candidate all the way to the pedestal of the Worshipful Master located at the other end? Be cautious though, the chequered floor can create strange optical illusions, making it much harder to see properly...

Find solutions page 66

40　　　　　　　　　　　　　　　　　The Mysteries of Freemasonry

Puzzle 78

What is a Masonic fire?

What on earth are you doing with that bucket?

Erm... somebody told me to be ready for a fire???

Find solutions page 66

Puzzle 79

Hiram Abiff is a central character to Freemasonic Rituals. All candidates get to know him quite well from the lectures on Traditional History.

Which of the following expression(s) can be used by Freemasons when they refer to him?

- A. The widow's son
- B. Our Master
- C. The Grand Architect
- D. The Grand Master
- E. The Chief Architect
- F. The Grand Geometrician

Puzzle 80

After a meeting, Freemasons share a meal and some good social time during what they call the Festive Board.

This is somewhat an extension of the main Lodge meeting. As such, it remains quite formal. For instance, it includes a few toasts.

Brothers start by a toast to the Queen (in England) and to the Craft itself, following which they honour the most prominent members of Grand Lodge in general and of their Lodge in particular.

Then, at 9pm, comes a very special toast.

Who is the 9 o'Clock toast dedicated to?

Find solutions page 66

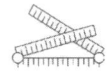

Puzzle 81 - Word Search

Can you identify some famous Freemasons in the grid below?

```
K X P O K D Z J F A H W R F V A X W O T
M J N C Z W J L E C H A I M W M R X E W
G I Y R F Z E F C P V H X C W T H Z O B
G I K R Z B H A K I O Z G E Y W X I C V
Z I V W F P Z P L O O P T V E S F S N N
E Z I O L C I O E T C U G Q Q G C Y M N
N Y E N J Y B U F F A L O B I L L O O B
H O U D I N I Y P D I N B H T N R T T S
W Q T L L I H C R U H C N D I O G W P T
I Y X G U B Y O R O G L C A O N H R Y K
L B H E N O S K C A J O W S I N E C Z I
D M E L L I N G T O N T E H L V R K L H
E F N F V W L I D V Q V S F E L T N F A
I T F R A N K L I N E A V R M O Z A R T
U V V S F B H W E L W U E A I E P B F J
C Q P G G Q O G T W Q C Y A X Z T R L P
T O W A O K O T P T R U M A N D V U G B
S G D B X B V V C N D S P S G Q G B J J
K P Q L S R E L L E S O D L K Q J P O E
M L C E P W R K T B V C Y W H K M U W D
```

Bolivar	Hoover	Scott
BuffaloBill	Houdini	Sellers
Burbank	Jackson	Truman
Churchill	Mozart	Twain
Ellington	Pope	Washington
Franklin	Revere	Wellington
Gable	Roosevelt	Wilde

Find solutions page 66

The Mysteries of Freemasonry

Puzzle 82

Back in medieval time, who started Freemasonry?

    A. Jacques De Molay
    B. Dan Brown
    C. The Sinclair (Saint-Clair) family
    D. That secret has long been lost

Puzzle 83

How many Freemasons are there in the world?

Puzzle 84

Freemasonic rituals places the origin of the world at 4000 B.C.

    Who established this date and in what conditions?

Puzzle 85

Which of these classic bathrooms items were invented by a Freemason?

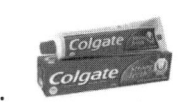

A.   B.   C.   D.

Find solutions page 67-68

Puzzle 86

A Masonic Lodge is supported by three pillars.

Each pillar displays a particular architectural style and denotes a specific human quality. They are also associated with an essential character from Masonic Traditional History as well as one of the three principal officers.

Using the 4 sets below, can you draw the link between the architectural style, the quality, the historical character and the principal officer?

Link each set together, for example:

Style — Officer   Character — Quality

Style

Ionic
Corinthian
Doric

Character

Hiram Abiff
King Solomon
King Hiram of Tyre

Officer

Worshipful. Master
Junior Warden
Senior Warden

Quality

Strength
Beauty
Wisdom

Find solutions page 68

The Mysteries of Freemasonry 45

Puzzle 87

The famous site of Stonehenge in Wiltshire, U.K., is somehow linked to Freemasonry.

Can you explain what this peculiar connection is?

Puzzle 88

After the Grand Lodge of England was formed in 1717, which country saw the next Grand Lodge?

Puzzle 89

Where was the Scottish Rite first implemented?

Hint: *Don't be fooled.*

Find solutions page 68-69

46 | The Mysteries of Freemasonry

Puzzle 90

Which of these tools and instruments can be found in a Lodge?

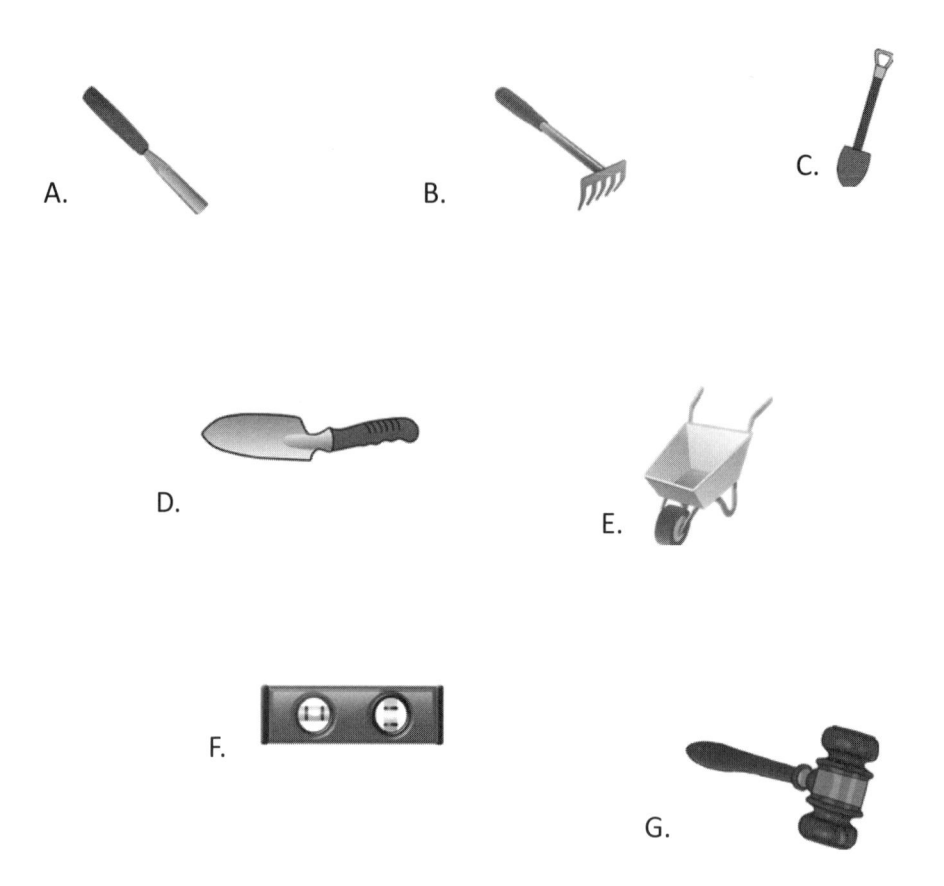

A.

B.

C.

D.

E.

F.

G.

Puzzle 91

Some jewels in the Lodge are called moveable, for instance: the level and the plumb rule.

Why the name *moveable*?

Find solutions page 69

The Mysteries of Freemasonry 47

Puzzle 92

What is Jacob's ladder?

Puzzle 93

Which of the following fast food does a Freemason eat (if any)?

A. McDonalds

B. KFC

C. Fish & Chips

D. Subway

E. Burger King

F. Kebab

Puzzle 94

Which of the following are not allowed during Lodge meetings?

A. Religious discussion
B. Political debate
C. Bringing a goat
D. Phone conversation

Find solutions page 69

Puzzle 95

Who am I?

Irish by birth, I studied medical science in London but refused to be a doctor. Instead, I joined the merchant navy at 16 and qualified as a master mariner in 1898. I was initiated into *Navy Lodge No. 2612* in 1901 but became too busy to attend meetings. Instead, I explored both the North and South poles and made important discoveries. There, during one particularly difficult expedition, my ship got caught in the ice. After almost 500 days, I finally managed to bring the crew to solid ground. I was knighted in 1909. I died of a heart attack in 1922.

Puzzle 96

Freemasonry doesn't accept cowans. An important part of the role of the Tyler is to protect the Lodge against their intrusion.

Why is that? And what is a cowan?

Find solutions page 70

The Mysteries of Freemasonry

Puzzle 97

Was Charles Darwin a Freemason?

Puzzle 98

Where can you meet a fellow Freemason?

Hint: *Think about one of the jewels... and a common expression.*

Puzzle 99

Some pubs in London seem to have an interesting Masonic connection.

Out of the five pubs below, can you spot the odd one out and explain why?

    A. Goose and Gridiron in St. Paul's Church-yard
    B. Crown in Parker's Lane
    C. City Pride in Farringdon
    D. Apple Tree in Covent Garden
    E. Rummer and Grapes in Westminster

Find solutions page 70

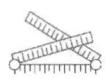

Puzzle 100 - Scrambled words

To help the new Entered Apprentices remember the various offices and members of the Lodge, the Mentor has brought a set of letters from a game of Scrabble.

He has put the letters in individual piles and has asked the new brothers to assemble them correctly.

    Can you help them out?

  A. eidsr nnaorwe

                          B. rfhurwpl miseasot

        C. frltecfwlao

                  D. jedu inonaroc

            E. waetdrs

Puzzle 101

If you have followed the quest correctly and ended up here after answering the 7 questions, congratulations, you have done a great job.

As a last generic question and a chance to win additional points, can you explain why the number 7 is important to Freemasonry?

Add an extra point for each correct answer.

Find solutions page 70

Congratulations!

You have now completed all the puzzles.

Solutions

Let's complete the quest first.

The answers to each puzzle of the quest, starting with number 3, also give you the next question of the quest. And so the trail is:

3 – 17 – 21 – 33 – 47 – 13 – 24 – 101

The bonus question was about the special significance of the number 7. Give yourself an extra point for each correct one.

1. There are 7 liberal arts.
2. 7 brethren are required to open or work a Lodge: The Master, two Wardens, two Fellowcraft and two Entered Apprentices.
3. It took 7 years to build the Temple of King Solomon.
4. 7 is also the sum of 3 + 4, 3 representing the triangle and 4 the square. Both figures bear great importance in Freemasonry.
5. The Ancients considered 7 as the number of totality. It was a symbol of the union of body and soul, or Heaven and Earth.
6. There are 7 stars represented on the first Tracing Board.
7. During the Raising ceremony (third degree), the candidate is asked to take 7 steps.

And now, turn to next page for all answers and explanations.

1

The cubit seems to originate in ancient Egypt. A typical cubit was measured as the distance between the tip of the middle finger and the elbow.

The man used for such measure was usually the principal architect on the construction. This means cubits may actually vary from project to project.

When the Romans came to use this prime unit of length, they couldn't accept the element of confusion, and therefore they standardised it to what would nowadays be 21.6 inches or 54.86 cm.

2 C.

The original lodges were temporary wooden workshops set alongside the building under construction and where the masons would work, dress and carve individual stones ready to be set in place. They may also have used them to rest.

3

Modern Freemasonry is assumed to have started when 4 London based lodges came together to form the first Grand Lodge in the year 1717.

4

The text says:
Many of the symbols used in Freemasonry find their origin in medieval operative stonemasonry. At a time when literacy was still very rare, teaching was mostly done via symbols and allegories. An Allegory is a story that can convey moral meanings, like a metaphor. Freemasonry is veiled in allegories, which means that you get to see more symbols and understand the allegories better as you progress through the degrees. In this sense, Freemasonry requires candidates to be patient and keen to develop their own knowledge and sense of morality.

5

In general terms, the son of a Freemason is called a Lewis.

6

The cypher used by freemason is also called Pigpen cypher. It uses a direct monoalphabetic substitution, meaning that each letter is replaced by a symbol.

Dots are said to represent pigs resting in their pen.

7

I am the Tyler. A possible origin of the word is that the last things builders did was to close the roof by posing tiles. By extension, the word became tyle.

The Tyler duties acts like the tiles on a rooftop by keeping the Lodge closed and impenetrable.

The Mysteries of Freemasonry - Solutions

The Tyler is often a member of the Lodge but doesn't have to be. It is indeed very often a paid job.

8
The cypher says:
I hope you are enjoying this book

9 B.
During his initiation, a new brother is taught how essential Benevolence and Charity are to Freemasonry. Truly the two best ornaments.

10
Operative masons used to wear gloves to protect their hands while working. The colour white is an indication of innocence and purity.

11
It is Solomon's temple.

12

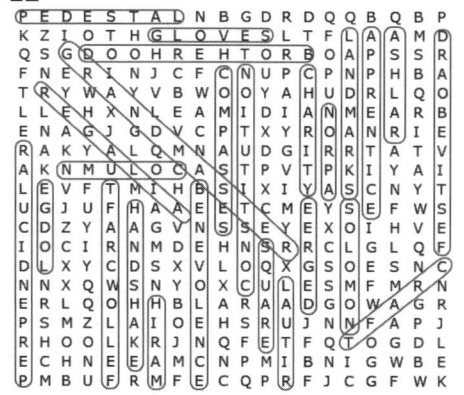

[word search grid]

13
The Masonic gauge is 24 inches long to represent the 24 hours in a day.

14
The only secrets in Freemasonry are the traditional signs, tokens and words that are used as a test of membership and allow Freemasons to show that they are indeed true Brothers.

There is a set of signs, tokens and words for each of the three degrees.

The signs and tokens are literally salutation and handshakes, while the words are, as you would guess, passwords!

And nothing else about Freemasonry is such a secret.

15
That's right: all of them!
Beethoven: strong presumption he was a member of a Lodge in Bonn - several pieces of his work carry very strong Masonic influence.
Mozart: *"Zur Wohltätigkeit"* ("Beneficence"), Vienna, Austria
Liszt: *"Zur Einigkeit"* (Unity), in Frankfort-on-the-Main, Germany
Haydn: *"Zur wahren Eintracht"* (True Concord), Vienna, Austria
Sibelius: *Soumi Lodge*, No.1 in Helsinki, Finland

16 C.
The Google mail logo represents an envelope. Envelopes have been used as a symbol for eMail since the creation of the service. There is nothing Masonic there.

The dollar bill figures the Great

Seal of the United States. Rumours and theories abound but there is no evidence to suggest the Great Seal, or indeed the dollar bill had a Masonic origin.

The Facebook logo shows the letter F as in... Facebook!

However, the other logo is used by the Widows Sons Masonic Bikers Association (WSMBA) in Bedfordshire.

A little something different from what the public usually associate with Freemasonry.

Check them out:

https://bedachapterwsmba.co.uk/

17
The minimum regular age to become a Freemason is 21.

18
The correct sentences are:
- Hiram Abiff, who is called our **Master** to all Freemasons, was the architect of Solomon's Temple.
- The **Worshipful Master** of the Lodge is installed every year to rule the Lodge.
- Every brother who has taken his third degree is entitled to be called a **Master Mason.**

19
I am the Cornucopia also called the horn of plenty.

20
The various aprons go as follows:

A. Fellowcraft

B. Royal Arch Companion

C. Craft Grand Officer

D. Mark Mason Master

E. Rose Croix

F. Knight Templar

G. Craft Past Master

The Mysteries of Freemasonry - Solutions

21
The Scottish Rite has 33 degrees.

22
After their rise to power in 1933, the Nazis made Freemasonry illegal. German Freemasons went underground to survive and they adopted the forget-me-not, possibly for its pale blue colour associated with the craft.

The flower was made into a lapel pin and serves today as a reminder of the oppression that drove the Order underground in the 20th century.

23
The two most prominent paths are the Scottish Rite (most common in the US) and the York rite (most prevalent in the UK).

To some extent, the Scottish Rite looks straightforward as a Freemason goes through 33 degrees. However, most brothers only access the 32nd degree. The 33rd is only granted by Grand Lodge.

The York rite, however, may offer more avenues to pursue a Masonic career. A Master Mason can choose to take his Royal Arch degree and then continue into another Order such as, for instance, the Knights Templar. He can also decide to join the Mark Masons and then the Fraternity of Royal Ark Mariners. These are just some examples.

The York Rite offers some diversity in the various Appendant Bodies one can join.

A final note: there are 3 main degrees in Freemasonry and a 33rd degree brother is no higher than any other Master Mason (3rd degree).

24
It is rule 101 which states:
The Master shall produce [the warrant of constitution] at every meeting of the Lodge.

25
Charade:
- My first is not low: high
- My second is a ram
- My third is the letter A, but pronounced like Ah!
- My fourth is beef (a cow when alive)

And my whole is **high-ram-ah-beef**

Hiram Abiff, the Chief Architect of Solomon's temple and the original Master to all Freemasons.

26
The master of a Lodge occupies the **Chair of Solomon,** a symbol that he is now the ruler of the Lodge.

27
That is a great story. And there are elements to consider here. Washington D.C. was designed by Pierre Charles L'enfant. And yes, L'enfant was initiated into Freemasonry in 1789, the year before the official foundation of the city.

L'Enfant studied arts in France and had a vision for a grandiose city to be both the permanent seat of the Government and the home of the President of the United States. He was born and raised in Paris, and no doubt took with him inspiration from the French capital design.

L'enfant was likely influenced by his knowledge of Arts, his birthplace Paris and Landmarks such as the

Palace of Versailles and its garden (the design of which predates. Freemasonry by a good century).

Actually, if you look at a plan of Versailles' gardens, you can make out the shape of compasses and square – a symbol that did not exist when André Le Nôtre designed the layout of the magnificent royal park.

Let's also remind ourselves that the Founding Fathers, including George Washington himself, drew inspiration for the U.S. capital city from the Italian grandiose town of Rome.

I am afraid there is no historical record proving any influence of Freemasonry over the design of Washington D.C. One can, however, find records of Freemasons laying the cornerstone for many of its significant buildings.

For instance, on September 18, 1793, President Washington himself, accompanied by three Worshipful Masters, conducted the cornerstone ceremony for the construction of the Capitol.

There is no doubt that Freemasonry was very present during the early years of the United States. Yet, one must remain cautious and keep to proven historical records rather than fall into the easy trap of attributing everything to Freemasonry simply because it uses some classic geometrical shapes.

Christian faith, English traditions, ideas from the Age of Enlightenment, even the French Revolution were influential in building this new and progressive country known as the U.S.A.

28
Hiram Abiff, the Chief Architect of Solomon's Temple and referred to as the Master by Freemasons, was the son of a widow.

All Master Masons are very closely associated with the Master Hiram Abiff, and by extension, they are also called "son of a widow".

It Is known that Freemasons can request the assistance of a brother by asking: *"Is there no hope for a widow's son?"*

29 C.
The pneumatic tyre was invented by Scottish Freemason John Boyd Dunlop in 1887. He was initiated in the *Lodge of Harmony No.111* in Belfast, Ireland.

30
The ceremony of the third and last degree, named The Raising, re-enacts the death of the Chief Architect of Solomon's Temple, Hiram Abiff and how his body was raised to be given a more appropriate sepulture.

The demise of Hiram Abiff is used as an allegory to reflect on one's own end.

31
Sir Alexander Fleming was initiated in 1909 into *Sancta Maria Lodge No 2682* and later joined *Lodge Misericordia No 3286.*

While he was studying the influenza virus, a mistake was made by which the wrong set of dishes were used. This lead him to discover penicillin.

He won the Nobel Prize in Medicine in 1945.

The Mysteries of Freemasonry - Solutions

32
All Freemasons are also called **Speculative Masons**.

This indicates that they are symbolic masons, developing their moral instead of constructing buildings.

33
Euclid proposition 47, also called Pythagorean theorem, states that:

In right-angled triangles the square on the side opposite the right angle equals the sum of the squares on the sides containing the right angle.

Illustration bellow.

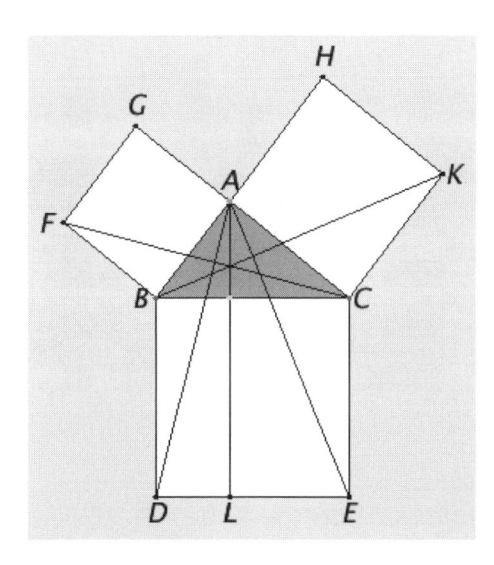

34
Logic Game.
The journalist is the brother from Northumberland.

The full details are listed in the table on the right.

	1	2	3	4	5
Province	London	Wiltshire	North Wales	Northumberland	Suffolk
Apron color	Light blue	Red	Pink	Dark blue	Beige
Drinks	Proseco	Orange juice	Coffee	Tea	Red wine
Profession	Police officer	Teacher	Bricklayer	Journalist	Barister
Office in the Lodge	Junior Warden	Senior Deacon	Secretary	Mentor	none

35
General John Pershing was a member of *Lincoln Lodge No. 19*, Lincoln, Nebraska.

36
In regular Craft, there are 3 degrees. The last one is called Master Mason. From there, a brother will trade the cream apron for a pale blue one that will distinguish him as a Master Mason.

37
Da Vinci died in 1519, almost 2 centuries before the first Grand Lodge was formed in 1717.

Da Vinci's work shows great knowledge and indeed admiration for geometry and perfection.

His Vitruvian man, a man at the centre of a circle, also inscribed in a square, could almost figure a Masonic symbol. One can imagined that if he had lived in the 18th century, he would likely have become a brother.

38
Let's face it, the Knights Templar inspire amazing stories. Beside, any connection to the Freemason ads to the entertainment.

The only authentic fact here is the date of the Knights Templar fall, a famous Friday 13th. Everything else written in the puzzle is just fictitious.

There is no record, no historical proof of any link between the two Orders.

Although Knights Templar exists today and are recognised by UGLE, they do not have a connection to the original Templars.

Actually, the earlier account of modern Masonic Knights Templar comes from a document dating back to 1778. It was then an Appendant Degree to Freemasonry.

As to what happened between 1307 and 1778, and whether there would be any connection between the historical and the modern Knights Templar, it is essentially speculation and guesswork.

39
You can say they are "**on the level.**"

40
Crossword resolved below.
The hidden word was **Apprentice**.

C	O	L	U	M	N		D	O	R	I	C		B
R		E			O		E				H		O
A		W		A	R	E	A		M		A		A
F	A	I	T	H		D		C	H	A	I	R	
T		S		O		E		O		G		G	O	D
			A	P	P	R	E	N	T	I	C	E	
C	O	R	N	E	R		N		E		H		E
O			C		I		T	Y	M	P	A	N	U	M
M	O	N	I	E	S		E		P		R		B
P			E		E	R	R		L		I		L
A	T	O	N	E	D			F	E	S	T	I	V	E
S			T			H		R			Y		M
S	O	O	S		T	Y	L	E	R		S	W	
E				P		M		E			U		J
S	O	L	O	M	O	N		J	O	I	N	E	D

41
I am sir Winston Churchill (1874 – 1965). Prime Minister of the United Kingdom between 1940-1945 and again in 1951-1955.

42
The answer is **craft**.
Freemasonry was very much inspired by real stone masons from medieval time. As these operative masons were learning their trade,

The Mysteries of Freemasonry - Solutions

they started as apprentices and progressed through the ranks or grades as their proficiency improved. Freemasonry has maintained this structure of learning a craft through its progressive degrees.

43 B.
Samuel Colt invented the revolver which still bears his name. He was a member of *St. Johns Lodge* in Hartford, Connecticut.

44
This is one of the common fallacies against Freemasonry, the idea that there is an overarching structure controlling it and subsequently the world on a global scale. But, no, there isn't.

The Grand Lodge is the ruling structure for a specific location such as a country or state.

Although Grand Lodges must recognise each other to allow members to visit, it doesn't mean one can rule over the others. Grand lodges are independent and sovereign.

45
Operative Freemasonry refers to stonemasons during the Middle Ages.

They were constructing cathedrals among other buildings. Unlike many workers (for instance in the fields), masons were not servants and did not belong to a Lord. This is why they were "free".

46
Historically, most of the operative stone cutters could not read, and therefore, images were used to teach them either about the trade or stories from the Bible.

During the growth of speculative Freemasonry, symbols were maintained as a means of teaching moral lessons. As an example, the level represents equality among men.

Teaching through images is the reason for stained glasses and adorned columns in churches.

47
After four years of negotiation, the two Grand Lodges in England united on 27 December 1813 to form the United Grand Lodge of England. This union led to a great deal of standardisation of ritual, procedures and regalia.

48
By this round, you should have only one remaining option for each card. You can confidently claim that the murder was committed in the **East** by the **Junior Deacon** with a **Gavel**.

49
Mozart became a freemason in Vienna in December 1784. He also composed music for Masonic purpose, especially the Masonic Funeral March.

50
In Latin, Quatuor Coronati means the Four Crowned Martyrs. The Crown here is symbolic of their martyrdom.

The legend has taken a variety of contradictory forms, but at its core lies this story: some sculptors working for Roman emperor Diocletian were asked to carve a pagan figure but refused to do so because of their Christian faith (which forbid them to produce any image of a pagan deity). Four soldiers refused to execute them for a similar reason. For their refusal, they were all executed.

The *Lodge Quatuor Coronati, No. 2076*, is a Masonic Lodge founded in 1886 in London and dedicated to Masonic research.

The Lodge was created by 9 Masons who had become very frustrated at the way the history of Freemasonry had expanded into the territory of wild speculations. They insisted that an evidence-based approach should be used in studying the past of the Order.

The Lodge members are active researchers and lecturers and include the majority of the Prestonian Lecturers, the only Masonic lectures given under the authority of the UGLE.

51
Individuals who have made a significant contribution to society and are held in very high regards can be chosen by the Grand Master of a Grand Lodge to be made a Master Mason through a single condensed ceremony.

For instance, Jesse Jackson, an American Civil Rights Activist and collaborator to Dr Martin Luther King was made a Mason at sight.

52
A candidate for initiation must roll up his left trouser leg. This is to make his knee bare.

During the ceremony, the candidate will be asked to kneel at the altar (the Master's pedestal) to take a solemn obligation.

Nothing should come between the Earth and his body as he takes this obligation. Therefore his knee must be bare.

This symbol persists today and has become one of the most iconic aspects of the preparation of a candidate for his initiation.

53
The Order of the Eastern Star, established by Rob Morris is indeed open to both men and women. Men must be Master Masons and women must be a Mason's relative or have an active membership to some Freemason-affiliated women or girls associations.

54
They feature London's Freemason's hall located in Great Queen Street.

55
Crossword resolved below.

The Mysteries of Freemasonry - Solutions

The 7 liberal arts are:
Trivium (literary disciplines)
- Grammar
- Rhetoric
- Logic

Quadrivium (linked to Mathematics)
- Arithmetic
- Geometry
- Music
- Astronomy

56
Well, yes and no. The origin of the expression comes from a form of ballot where the voter uses a white ball to signify approval or a black one to reject.

Freemasonry has used such ballot since the very early 18th century and gave rise to the expression blackballing.

The first ballot for a Freemason takes place right before his initiation, to decide whether or not to accept him. So, should a black ball be revealed against him, he would not be approved and therefore would not become a Freemason.

57
The administrative unit of the Royal Arch is called Chapter. They are usually sponsored by a Lodge and sometimes share the same number.

58
LoI stands for Lodge of Instruction. It is a regular meeting where two things happen.
- First, the officers of the Lodge and other members prepare for the next meeting, especially the ritual part. If you compare a ceremony to a theatrical play, then the LoIs are the various rehearsals necessary to make it run smoothly.
- Then, after some good work, the brothers generally gather for drinks or dinner.

59
Cube B is the only one that can be constructed from the template

60
Boaz and Jachin were the two pillars at the entrance of King's Solomon temple. (Jeremiah 52:21-22 and Kings 7:13-22, 41-42)

61 B.
Sherlock Holmes creator, Arthur Conan Doyle was a Freemason.
He was initiated at the *Phoenix Lodge No. 257* in Southsea, Hampshire (UK) in 1887.

62
The first Grand Lodge was formed in London in 1717.

In 1751, a rival lodge claimed the original Grand Lodge was too modern whereas they represented the original rites.

This new Lodge called itself Antients and the first Lodge the Moderns.

After years of dismissing each other, the two Lodges finally came together in 1813 and formed the United Grand Lodge of England.

63
14 U.S Presidents were Freemason:
- George Washington
- James Monroe
- Andrew Jackson
- James Polk

- James Buchanan
- Andrew Johnson
- James Garfield
- William McKinley
- Theodore Roosevelt
- Howard Taft
- Warren Harding
- Franklin Roosevelt
- Harry Truman
- Gerald Ford

64

Edwin "Buzz" Aldrin was the second man to walk on the Moon in July 1969.

His walk was seen on television by over 600 millions people worldwide and became known as "the Moonwalk". Aldrin is a member of *Montclair Lodge No. 144* of New Jersey (U.S).

His mother's maiden name was Marion Moon. Sadly she passed away a few months before Aldrin set foot on the moon.

65

This is the city of London.

The great fire of 1666 damaged a large part of the town, and Sir Christopher Wren rebuilt 52 churches, including his masterpiece: St Paul's cathedral.

In 1717, the first Grand Lodge came in existence in a pub located very close to St Paul.

It has been speculated for a long time that Wren was a Freemason, but evidence remains elusive. It is however very likely that he has been accepted in an operative Lodge before speculative Freemasonry.

66

Captain Matthew Flinders (1774 - 1814) was initiated into the *Friendly Cultivator Lodge* on Mauritius.

He was the first to circumnavigate Australia and produce charts of the country.

The land had been named "Terra Australis Incognita" which means Unknown Southern Land. Flinders then called it **Australia**, thinking it was a much easier way to pronounce and remember the name.

67

Money and by extension any metals are not allowed during the ceremony of initiation.

In medieval times, metal was rare and often used as currency.

A candidate for Freemasonry must enter poor and divested of any metallic object.

68

Well, wouldn't it be nice if movies and novels were always true?

The one dollar bill features the Great Seal of the U.S. There is however no evidence of a Masonic origin to the Great Seal.

From 1776, several individuals presented their ideas for the Great Seal. It took three committees and six years before Congress asked Secretary Charles Thomson to come up with a final design. He combined elements from all three previous attempts.

The final version was approved in 1782. Inspirations came from existing European currencies, Biblical symbols and various representation of the number 13.

For instance, the broken pyramid

The Mysteries of Freemasonry - Solutions

is made of 13 levels representing the 13 original states that declared their independence from the British empire.

The Eye of Providence is first and foremost a Christian symbol. When used in Freemasonry, it is represented with a cloud. But it only appeared in 1797, a good 14 years after the creation of the Great Seal.

None of the individuals involved in the original design work were Masons. T

he alleged Masonic origin is none other than wishful thinking.

69
Crossword resolved below.

The motto of Freemasonry figures in the greyed out cells:
Audi Vide Tace

70

The dinner that follows a Lodge meeting is called the **Festive Board**.

71 B.
Wisdom, Strength and Beauty are the three pillars that support the Lodge.

72
The most famous Masonic symbol is formed by a square and compasses.

73
It is the ashlar. The rough and smooth ashlars are symbols of progressing through life by learning and experience.

74 A, B.
You have a choice:

Henry Ford was a Freemason; he was raised in Detroit, *Palestine Lodge No. 357*.

Walter Percy Chrysler was also a Freemason, member of *Apollo Lodge No. 297* in Kansas

75
All members of the Lodge are brothers and therefore equal. Titles and ranks from outside the Lodge have little to no value inside.

Because Paul is now a Past Master, Steve calls him Worshipful Brother. Steve having joined recently is called Brother.

One of the main attraction of Freemasonry throughout the ages is that it does not replicate the ranks and social position for the outside world.

In the Lodge, we are all brothers.

76

The three principal officers who rule the Lodge are the Worshipful Master, The Senior Warden and the Junior Warden.

77

The solution is shown below.

78

Firing a toast is a way to mark some respect.

Although the real origin of the Masonic fire has been lost in time, Lodges have long been using glasses with a heavy bottom for toasting. The "bang" made by these glasses as they are slammed down on the table replicates the fire of a gun.

Freemasons fire a toast with 21 volleys. This likely comes from a naval tradition whereby a ship entering a foreign harbour would fire its gun towards the sea to indicate it had no hostile intention. The firing of 21 shots has since become a sign of respect.

79 A, B, E.

The correct expressions are:
- The widow's son
- Our Master
- The Chief Architect

The Great Architect and Grand Geometrician (Of The Universe) make reference to the Supreme Being, or God.

The Grand Master is the Freemason ruling a Grand Lodge.

80

The 9 o'clock toast is dedicated to absent Brethren. It offers a way of remembering departed brothers and friends and to drink to their memory.

It is common that at 9pm, no matter where he is and what he is presently doing, a Freemason may raise a glass to a friend who has passed away.

81

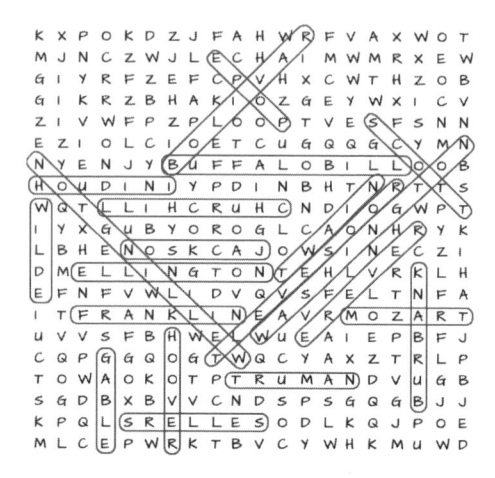

The Mysteries of Freemasonry - Solutions

- Simón Bolivar - *Lautaro Lodge,* Cádiz, Spain
- William Cody a.k.a Buffalo Bill - *Platte Valley Lodge No. 32,* Nebraska, U.S.
- Luther Burbank - *Santa Rosa Lodge No. 57,* in Santa Rosa, California, U.S.
- Winston Churchill - *Studholme Lodge No. 1591,* England
- Duke Ellington - *Social Lodge No. 1,* Washington, D.C., U.S.
- Benjamin Franklin - *St. John's Lodge* in Philadelphia, U.S.
- Clark Gable - *Beverly Hills Lodge No. 528*
- John Edgar Hoover - *Federal Lodge No. 1,* Washington D.C., U.S.
- Harry Houdini - *St. Cecile Lodge No. 568,* New York, U.S.
- Jesse Jackson - *Grand Lodge of Illinois,* U.S.
- Wolfgang Amadeus Mozart - *Zur Wohltätigkeit Lodge (Beneficence),* Vienna, Austria
- Alexander Pope - P*remier Grand Lodge of England*
- Paul Revere - Most Worshipful Grand Master of *The Grand Lodge of Massachusetts,* U.S.
- Franklin Delano Roosevelt - *Holland Lodge, No. 8,* New York City, U.S.
- Sir Walter Scott - *Canongate Kilwinning from Leith, Lodge 36,* Scotland
- Peter Sellers - *Chelsea Lodge No 3098*
- Harry Truman - *Belton Lodge No. 450* in Belton, Missouri, U.S.
- Mark Twain - *Polar Star Lodge No. 79,* St. Louis, U.S.
- George Washington - Lodge in Fredericksburg, Virginia. He was also the Grand Master of the Grand Lodge of Virginia, U.S.
- Arthur Wellesley, Duke of Wellington - *Trim Dublin Lodge 494,* Ireland
- Oscar Wilde - *Apollo Masonic Lodge* - Oxford University, England

82 D.
In truth, nobody knows precisely when and how Freemasonry started.

- Jacques de Molay was the 23rd Grand Master of the Knights Templar. When the order was disbanded, he was arrested, tried and subsequently burnt in 1314. He was the last Grand Master.
- Dan Brown is the author of successful novels including the Da Vinci Code and The Lost Symbol (which explores U.S. Masonic lore)
- The Sinclair or Saint Clair were at the origin on the Roslin Chapel foundation in 1446. In 1736, William Saint Clair of Roslin became the first Grand Master Mason of Scotland. A lot of speculation connects them to the Templars, but this story is for another day.

83
There is an estimated 6 million Freemasons worldwide.

They are about 2 million in the U.S. alone and about 200.000 in England and Wales.

84
In the latter part of 17th century Britain, the Church sought to re-establish its authority.

It denied the work of science and claimed that all knowledge could be derived from the Bible alone.

Looking to assess the actual age of the world, and in a twist of irony, the Church of England turned to the Royal Society: a body created in 1660 to advance scientific knowledge. Its president at the time, Sir Isaac Newton couldn't resist the challenge.

He calculated the age of the world by using the lineage from the book of Genesis. This lead him to speculate the date of Creation to be 4000 B.C.

This is called Anno Lucis, the "Year of Light".

Freemasonry uses this date in various official documents.

For instance, a Master Mason's certificate issued in the year 2019 will be dated A.L. 6019.

85 A, D.
A bar of Sunlight soap and a Gillette razor.

The bar of soap was created by William Lever and his brother James in 1885.

William Lever was initiated in 1902. The Lodge was renamed after him: *The William Hesketh Lever Lodged No. 2916*, U.S.

King Camp Gillette was also a Freemason, raised in *Adelphi Lodge* in Quincy, Massachusetts in 1901.

86
The solution in picture in the next column.

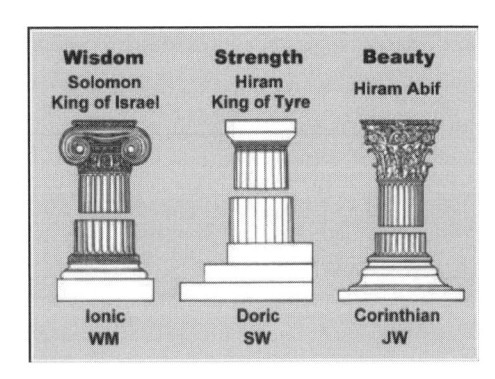

Wisdom	Strength	Beauty
Solomon	Hiram	Hiram Abif
King of Israel	King of Tyre	
Ionic	Doric	Corinthian
WM	SW	JW

87
By the early 20th century, the Antrobus family had owned the land on which Stonehenge stood for a considerable time.

In 1915, the heir died at war and the remaining family members decided to sell the 35 acres of land at an auction in Salisbury.

A Freemason named Cecil Chubb bought the plot of land to avoid it falling in foreign hands and gave it to his wife. They gifted it to the British government in 1918 on the proviso that no building would be constructed within 400 yards and that the price to visit would be low.

Chubb was subsequently made Baronet of Stonehenge.

He was initiated in the *Lodge Elias de Derham, No. 586,* on 26 October 1905.

Legend has it that he only went to the auction to buy some chairs...

88
Ireland's Grand Lodge formed in 1725.

It was followed by Scotland's Grand Lodge in 1736.

Don't forget that England then also included Wales, there has therefore never been a Grand Lodge for Wales.

The Mysteries of Freemasonry - Solutions

89
Not in Scotland! The Scottish Rite originated in France but only formally started with the creation of the Mother Supreme Council in Charleston, South Carolina – U.S. in May 1801.

Although it took inspiration from the various degree systems already in use across Europe at that time, it properly started in the U.S. and grew from there.

90 A, D, F, G.
The level, the chisel, the gavel and the trowel are Masonic tools or jewels.

91
The moveable jewels are the emblems of some officers in the Lodge.

They are passed onto the new officers when they are appointed. Thus, they move from brother to brother.

In opposition, the Tracing Board and the rough and perfect ashlars are immoveable jewels. They remain firmly in position for the brothers to reflect on their meanings.

92
In Genesis 28:10-19, Jacob has a dream where he sees a ladder set on the Earth and reaching to Heaven.

In Freemasonry, the ladder is used as a symbol of moral and intellectual progress. It is associated with the Plumb Rule as a symbol of rectitude and truth.

It is mostly depicted standing on the Volume of Sacred Law to indicate how the teaching of the Bible can help us ascend to Heaven.

93 B.
Long before creating the restaurant franchise that would make his silhouette known to the world, KFC, Colonel Harland Sanders was initiated in 1917 in Indiana.

He later became affiliated with *Hugh Harris Lodge No. 938* in Kentucky.

94
All of them:
- All electronic devices must be switched off.
- Freemasons are told at their initiation to avoid political or religious discussions.
- And goats... really, you still believe in that old hoax?

One possible origin of the legend of goats in Freemasonry is found in the name given to the Supreme Being or God in the first degree: the

Great Architect Of The Universe or GAOTU, which obviously looks a bit like the word goat.
Another source is Baphomet. The Knights Templar were supposed to worship this idol, yet the name never appears in any historical records.
In 1854, a French occultist named Eliphas Levi, drew Baphomet as a goat to represent the universe in the form of binary opposites.

95
Ernest Shackleton (1874-1922).

96
Cowans are profanes, intruders and eavesdroppers. They are non-Masons who attempt to obtain the secrets by ruse or force. The Tyler's sword is to deter or fight them.

97
Darwin's father Robert and grandfather Erasmus were both Freemasons, but there is no record of Charles Darwin being one himself.

98
"On the Square" or "on the Level".

99
The City Pride is the odd one out. The four others were the meeting spots of the four Lodges that formed the first Grand Lodge in 1717.

100
The scrambled words read:
  A. Senior Warden
  B. Worshipful Master
  C. Fellowcraft
  D. Junior Deacon
  E. Steward

Give yourself 1 point for every correct answer and solved puzzle.

In the end, add all points.

75 to 100 points
Gold Medal
Are you a Worshipful Brother?
You certainly know your Freemasonry.

50 to 75 points
Bronze Medal
You must be a Master Mason already.

25 to 50 points
Silver Medal
It was a worthy effort.

Under 25 points
Did you even try?

Thank you for playing along.
I hope to see you in the next puzzle book.

Back cover maze solution.